AMIE A RICH

Beyond NUMBING

HOW SELF-LOVE HEALS THE WOUNDS WE HIDE

ISBN: 978-1-971349-43-5

Dedication

To my children,

You were the reason I chose courage when staying would have been easier.

Walking away was never simple, but the truth was undeniable: you deserved a mother who was happy, present, and fully available in every way.

I followed the knowing in my heart, the inner guidance that whispered, the cycle ends with you. Even before I had the language for it, breaking generational trauma was never just my healing, it was my promise to you.

And to the little girl I once was—the brave, overburdened mini-me who carried the weight of a world she never should have been asked to hold, who had to become strong long before she ever felt safe—I'm finally giving her the gentleness, protection, and permission to rest that she has always deserved.

This book is for my children, and for me, the grown woman and the inner child healing together, rewriting our story, and choosing a future where the patterns end, and love leads the way.

Table of Contents

Foreword

For her, for me, for them.

My mom did not watch movies. That was a little-known fact around the house. If there was a movie coming out that we wanted to watch, we knew Mom would not be watching it with us. We would always ask her and poked fun at her when she'd say no. She always said no. We were so unaware of what was really going on. I never knew where she would go during these movie nights: maybe she was at the computer, or in the kitchen, or cleaning something, but all I knew was that she was elsewhere. What seemed like merely a distaste for cinema turned out to be a woman's struggle to slow her ever-racing mind that was bubbling over with daily demands. Never would I have imagined that something so comical and small to my young mind would be a struggle I would relate to so much as an adult. The responsibility of being there for so many people is overwhelming when your own needs are not met. Responsibility plays a main role in this dilemma: if I stop moving for even a second, everything I've been keeping perfectly in orbit would implode, leaving me and everyone I love drifting off into the mess of debris that *I* allowed to happen.

I first noticed people-pleasing tendencies in myself in high school. I was familiar with this concept because I had talked about it with my mother prior, and she speaks a lot about that in this book. However, talking about all the ways people-pleasing showed up in everyday life didn't prepare me for when it showed up in more subtle ways. I was always saying "*yes*" to things, and I would walk from class to class with a huge ball of stress in the center of my chest, worried about making everyone happy. It was effortless to put others first and take care of my friends, and at no cost to me, but when saying "*yes*" all the time began to battle with my peace, I knew something wasn't right. Even after I realized what my tendencies were, I kept up the same routines. It was easier to keep giving my time and energy to aid someone else, and for a very long time it took no real toll. So I thought, *Why not?* I realized this was a big problem when the thought of disappointing someone, letting down someone I committed to, began to feel paralyzing. As soon as I wouldn't allow myself to be put first, I knew, *this isn't how it's supposed to be.*

Reading my mother's own words, about her journey through healing her inner child and choosing herself, has given me the language to talk about my own struggles and think about how things affect me and my body. Looking inward at how my nervous system reacts to external impulses has told me a lot about the things I hold within. There is no finish line for work like this; We are all learning more every day. But curiosity is the first step, and language enables that curiosity.

Within the last few years, my memory has gotten noticeably worse. Slowly, I wouldn't be able to remember little things, or I would not remember the previous week's events, and finally one day I was unable to recollect what I had done yesterday. I had not thought about why I was experiencing this until I read this book and found similarities within myself. My journey into regulating my nervous system and being present has given me the tools I need to dive into the ways my body is trying to survive, and why my memory may be a sacrifice to that survival.

I wish you all the peace that I know you're searching for as you pick up this book. And I ask you to remember as you continue with your day and with your life, that we are all doing *it* for the first time, be gentle with yourself, and be understanding above all.

To you, to them, and to theirs.

With the warmest of my regards,
McKenna Hill

Foreword

by Hanna Olivas

There are books that educate. Books that inspire. Books that challenge us to think differently. And then there are books like this one, books that reach into your chest, place a hand over your heart, and remind you that you are still alive beneath everything you had to carry.

From the moment I met Amie Rich, I knew she was a woman whose story wasn't just meant to be spoken, it was meant to be felt. She is one of the rare ones, the ones who walk into a room and bring both truth and tenderness with them. Not because life has been easy, but because she had to learn how to rebuild herself from the inside out.

Amie spent decades doing what so many women do: Surviving. Performing. Holding it all together while quietly unraveling under the weight of inherited trauma, impossible expectations, burnout, and silence. Like countless women, she learned to numb long before she learned to feel. She learned to function long before she learned to heal. And yet even through the numbness, there was a whisper inside her that said, There is more for you. There always has been.

What you hold in your hands is that "more."

This book is not written from theory, nor from rehearsed wisdom. It is written from lived experience, cellular-level healing, spiritual awakening, and the holy work of coming back home to yourself. It is written by a woman who spent years climbing the corporate ladder only to realize she had abandoned her inner world in the process, a woman who finally turned inward, listened to her soul, and said, No more. The cycle ends here.

Amie is a high-performance coach, a spiritual hypnotherapist, and a nervous system practitioner, but before any of those titles existed, she was a woman searching for her truth, her freedom, and her voice. And she found it, not in grand gestures, but in the sacred, gritty, beautiful small steps of healing. In breathwork. In journaling. In grief. In boundaries. In forgiveness. In facing the parts of herself she once hid. In choosing to feel again.

Her healing journey became her calling, and this book is the offering born from that calling.

As her "About the Author" page beautifully states, she guides others "on their journey from survival to self-love", and every chapter in this book is a pathway toward that same transformation.

What makes Beyond Numbing extraordinary is that it doesn't preach. It doesn't demand. It doesn't tell you who to be. Instead, it sits beside you, the way Amie herself sits beside the women she serves and it says,

Here is truth. Here is tenderness. Here is the voice you lost.

Here is the freedom you forgot you deserved.

This book gives language to experiences so many women have endured in silence. It reminds us that numbness is not failure, it is an intelligent response to pain. It is the body protecting us. It is the spirit surviving. And healing is not about shaming the numbness; it is about honoring the resilience that kept us alive long enough to choose something different.

Amie writes with honesty, vulnerability, and a spiritual depth that is unmistakable. She reminds us that healing is not a destination but a series of choices, the pause before reacting, the breath before speaking, the moment you choose truth instead of the old story.

She teaches us that coming home to ourselves is the bravest act of all.

If you are holding this book, you are holding a mirror, a companion, and a permission slip. You are holding the possibility of a life beyond survival. You are holding the invitation to finally feel, to finally be seen, to finally reclaim the parts of you that went quiet for too long.

And you are holding the heart of a woman who did the work deeply, fiercely, tenderly, and now extends her hand so you can walk your way out of numbing, too.

Amie often says that healing "radiates forward," transforming not only ourselves but the generations who follow. That truth echoes through every chapter.

I am honored to witness her journey.

I am honored to witness your courage as you begin your own.

And I am honored to introduce a book, and a woman who will help countless others step into a life they no longer need to numb just to survive.

Hanna Olivas
Publisher & Co-Founder, She Rises Studios
Las Vegas, Nevada

66

YOU DON'T HAVE TO
BREAK DOWN TO
WAKE UP.
BUT MAYBE YOU
ALREADY HAVE, AND
THAT'S WHY YOU'RE
HERE.

We live in a world that applauds our numbing. The busyness. The perfectionism. The people-pleasing. The way that we take care of everyone else before ourselves. On the outside, it looks like you're doing amazing. But inside? You're worn down. Disconnected. Whispering to yourself, "Is this really all there is?"

Numbing doesn't always look like falling apart. Sometimes it looks like being the strong one. The dependable one. The one who never slows down, never asks for help, never lets anyone see the cracks. You may not have called it numbing, but it kept you alive.

I once had a psychic reading where the woman asked me what the word "warrior" meant to me. I knew the word, of course, but I never thought of myself that way.

She looked at me and said, "You were badass."

I laughed and jokingly asked why she used past tense. She told me that in a past life, I was a warrior who defended my people and may have even died defending them.

Then she said, "You need to know you are a badass."

That landed in me in a way I didn't expect. Because while I may never carry a sword into battle, I do carry the same instinct to protect. To hold it all together. To be everything for everyone I love. And maybe that's why the word warrior never left me, because somewhere in my DNA, I've always believed it was my job to keep my people safe.

This book isn't about addiction. It's about the invisible armor you've been carrying to survive. The masks you've worn. The roles you've played. The parts of yourself you had to silence just to be loved or accepted.

Beyond Numbing is an invitation to lay all of that down. To come back to yourself. To rediscover the parts of you that were never broken, just hidden.

You don't need to be fixed. You don't need to keep proving your worth.

You just need to remember who you are.

And if you feel that tug inside—that knowing there's more to life than just surviving—you belong here.

Welcome home.

My Story

If you're reading this, I don't believe it's by accident. There's a reason that these words found their way to you. Maybe it's a quiet nudge, a whisper from your intuition, or a moment of divine timing that landed this book in your hands. I don't know exactly what part of your story you're carrying, but I do know this: you don't have to carry it alone. This is a space for truth, for softness, for remembering what you were never meant to forget; your worth, your voice, and your wholeness. I am sharing my story here, not because it matters more than yours, but because sometimes when we see ourselves reflected in someone else's healing, it gives us the courage to begin our own.

I grew up a military daughter. We moved around in my early years, though honestly, I don't remember much of that time. Just fragments, snapshots, that come to life through old photographs. My dad served in the Navy as a submariner, often gone for months at a time. He didn't speak much about what he experienced, but I know he was the torpedoman. I can only imagine the weight of carrying such responsibility. Being away from your family during your children's most tender years, while also holding the power to release something so destructive. That's a burden I couldn't grasp as a child, but now, as an adult, I hold that complexity with compassion.

Eventually, we settled in Southern California, and life got busy. Both of my parents worked. My mom coached my soccer and t-ball teams, always showing up, always on the go. I was active, too. After high school, I even taught soccer to seven, eight, and nine-year-olds. It's funny to think about that now, because these days I'm admittedly a little uncoordinated. I've become more of a "cheer-from-the-stands" kind of woman. Put me on a dance floor, and I'll lose the beat in no time—but hey, I'll laugh while doing it.

I have a younger brother. We are just three years apart, though I still call him my baby brother. We both carry our own stories, shaped by the same roots but branching in different directions. I've come to believe that some generational wounds are meant to be healed in this lifetime, while others unfold slowly, lesson by lesson, across lifetimes.

I grew up in a house where silence carried more weight than words. There was love, but also a quiet tension that hummed beneath the surface, unspoken but ever-present. My childhood was shaped by addiction, though I didn't have the language for it back then. My dad drank heavily, but we never called it what it was. We didn't talk about it. We just absorbed it. We became experts at keeping the peace, smoothing things over, and pretending everything was fine.

When I was in high school, my mom shared that she was gay. It wasn't a dramatic reveal—we had a brief conversation in the car, and that was that. I think it was her way of making it feel less disruptive. But for me, it stirred a wave of emotions I didn't know how to name: confusion, fear, uncertainty. Being gay wasn't something we talked about openly, and I didn't know how to hold that truth as her daughter. So, I did what I had always done. I tucked those feelings away.

That's how I learned the unspoken rules: don't make waves, don't need too much, don't feel too loudly.

And I adapted. I became who the environment needed me to be. I was the peacekeeper, the overachiever, the "good girl" who held it all together. On the outside, I looked steady and in control. But on the inside, I was just a child who had learned to survive by disconnecting from her own needs.

This is the truth about numbing. It doesn't always look like addiction. Sometimes it looks like perfectionism. Or people-pleasing. Or over-functioning. Or staying so busy you never have to feel. Sometimes it feels like being the strong one who never asks for help. I didn't reach for substances, but I numbed all the same. I numbed with achievement. I numbed with caretaking. I numbed with silence.

It took me decades to realize that the world had been rewarding my self-abandonment and calling it "success".

But this is not a book about addiction. It's a book about healing. About finally feeling safe enough to come home to yourself. It's about recognizing the trauma that taught you to disconnect from your own needs and beginning the slow, sacred work of reconnecting with the parts of you that got left behind. It's about learning how to regulate your nervous system, listen to your inner child, and reclaim your voice.

We'll explore what trauma really is, how it lives in the body, and the ways we learned to split from ourselves just to feel safe. We'll talk about nervous system regulation, inner child healing, and how to build a relationship with the Self that's rooted in compassion, not performance.

Because once you stop numbing, you start living. Not just surviving, but choosing, feeling, and existing in full color. And from that place, healing stops being about "getting better" and starts being about becoming whole.

You don't have to keep numbing.

You don't have to keep proving.

There is a truer version of you waiting to be uncovered, and she doesn't need to be fixed. She just needs to be loved.

She's been waiting.

Let's go meet her.

A Note Before You Begin

There are moments in life that don't announce themselves as turning points.

They arrive quietly.

In a pause.

In a reaction you didn't expect.

In the exhaustion that lingers even after you've rested.

This book was born from moments like those.

Not from one dramatic breaking point, but from many small realizations that slowly asked to be noticed.

Moments that made me see the ways I had learned to numb.

The ways I stayed busy, capable, and composed while parts of me quietly hid in the background.

You may recognize yourself in these pages.

Not because our stories are the same, but because the patterns are familiar.

The pushing through.

The staying strong.

The subtle disconnection that can exist even in a life that looks "successful" from the outside.

As you read, I want you to know this:

you will feel this book.

Some chapters may feel like relief, finally having language for something you've always sensed.

Others may stir discomfort, grief, or resistance.

That doesn't mean something is wrong.

It means something honest is being touched.

Each chapter builds on the last, gently guiding you through the same progression that helped me recognize what I was numbing... and why.

There is no rush here.
Pause when you need to.
Let the words settle in your body, not just your mind.

This is not therapy, and it is not about diagnosing or fixing you.
It is an invitation to awareness—
to understanding the survival strategies that once protected you,
and exploring whether they are still serving the person you are
becoming.

This work is raw, but it is not reckless.
It is honest, but it is held.

Empowerment doesn't come from bypassing what we feel.
It comes from staying present with it long enough to understand
ourselves with compassion instead of shame.

If emotions rise as you read, let them.
If you need space, take it.
Your nervous system knows the pace better than your mind ever could.

You haven't been hiding because you're broken.
You've been surviving.

This book is an invitation to stop numbing,
to gently turn toward what you've been avoiding,
and to begin coming home to yourself—one chapter at a time.

I'm honored to walk this part with you.

— **Amie**

A Note on Shame

Before we go any further, let's pause and name something that might already be bubbling up in you. I know it did for me while I wrote the words in this book.

Shame.

Shame for disconnecting.

Shame for not knowing.

Shame for coping in the only ways you knew how.

That tightness in your chest, or the voice in your head that whispers, "I should have done better".

Yeah, I've heard that voice too. Loud and clear. And here's what I've come to realize. Numbing is not a weakness. It's a wound response. A brilliant, adaptive strategy cooked up by a nervous system that was just trying to keep you safe.

There is no shame in surviving.

This book isn't here to judge you for how you've made it through. It's here to honor those survival strategies. To recognize the younger parts of you who learned early how to adapt, stay alert, stay useful, or stay quiet in order to belong. The parts of you who figured out how to function in chaos, who learned to read the room, carry the weight, or keep going when the waves felt too big to swim. They kept you afloat when you didn't yet have another choice. They did their job, and they did it well. But here's the good news, you don't have to stay in survival forever.

We're not here to shame the numbness. We're here to get curious about it. To understand it. To befriend and thank it. And then, gently, at your own pace, begin the sacred work of softening. Of reconnecting. Of feeling safe enough to feel again.

Naming the numb doesn't mean you're broken. It means you're brave. It means you're willing to look inward with honesty and compassion. It means you're ready to meet yourself with the tenderness you always deserved.

Every page that follows is a love letter, both to the strength it took to survive, and to the softness you're being called to reclaim.

A Soul Perspective

Lastly, before we begin this journey together, there's something I want to share, something I believe deep in my bones, and maybe you do too.

We are all here to learn.

Each of us comes into this life with a sacred lesson, something our soul chose to explore, to heal, to remember. And in the moment when we are born, we forget. That forgetting is part of the agreement. Because life is the journey back to remembering... that is where the growth happens.

I believe we choose our families, our experiences, our challenges—not as punishment, but as soul invitations. We choose the people who will walk alongside us in this lifetime, even if their roles are difficult or painful. Not because they're perfect, but because our soul recognizes what it came to learn.

I don't say this to bypass the very real pain many of us have endured. I say this because when I look back at my own story, I don't feel regret. I feel reverence. I believe my soul family came together with me for a reason. And sometimes, when I'm quiet enough, I wonder who played what role in lifetimes past. Maybe my father was once my son. Maybe I was my mother's mother. Maybe the ones who hurt me deeply came here to teach me strength, or softness, or both.

Seeing my life this way doesn't erase the pain. But it helps me hold it with more compassion. It reminds me that healing isn't just about mending what's broken. It's about remembering what's sacred. So, despite your belief on this topic, I ask you to see yourself as a divine soul on a journey of self-discovery.

And, as we walk through these pages together, I invite you to consider:

What if your journey isn't an accident?

What if your story holds more purpose than you've been told?

What if this, right here, is your remembering?

Beyond Numbing Sections

This book is written in sections, or stages, if you will. Just like a butterfly, your healing unfolds in stages.

The letters of **HOPE** aren't just steps in a process; they're the wings of your own becoming. Each section of this book is a piece of the butterfly's form, guiding you from the quiet strength of the caterpillar to the hidden transformation of the chrysalis, and finally into the open air of your own freedom. Even the caterpillar is beautiful, even the cocoon is sacred, because without them the wings would never form. The beauty isn't only in the flight. It's in the journey. It's in the remembering that everything you need for your transformation is already within you.

These pages will help you shed what no longer serves you, honor the wisdom that kept you safe, and awaken the wings that have been waiting to be freed. **HOPE** is your map, and as you move through each section, you're not becoming someone new—you're becoming who you were always meant to be. You are divinely guided, and this journey is your homecoming.

H – Honoring Your Numbing
O – Own the Cost
P – Pause
E – Embody the Freedom

WHAT
HAPPENED TO
YOU MATTERS.
HOW YOUR
BODY
REMEMBERED
IT MATTERS
MORE.

Part One – Honoring the Numbness

Before we heal, we have to see. Before we see, we have to be honest. That honesty isn't always loud. Sometimes it whispers through the busywork, the perfectionism, the zoning out. Sometimes it sounds like "I'm fine" when you're anything but.

This first piece of the butterfly is about awareness. "Honoring the Numbness" means recognizing that your survival strategies were never weakness. They were brilliant. They were the ways your nervous system kept you safe when life felt too overwhelming to feel.

Numbing is rarely as obvious as we expect it to be. Sometimes it looks like always being the one who holds it together. Or disappearing into daydreams. Or never letting anyone get too close.

Sometimes it's perfectionism, people-pleasing, or busyness. However numbing showed up for you, it was wisdom. It was survival. But survival isn't the same as living. And you're here now because you're ready for something more.

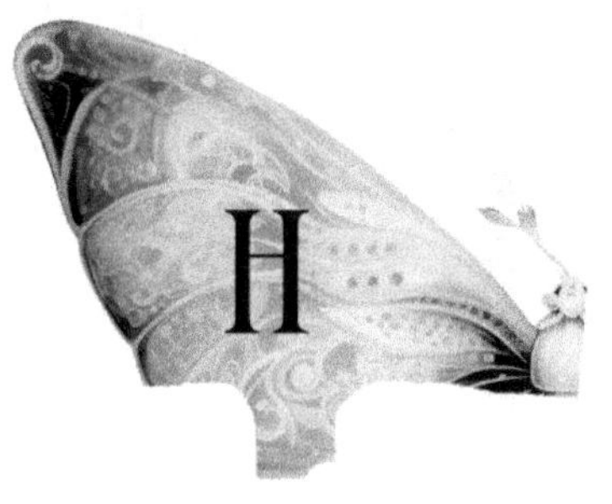 In this section, we'll explore what numbing really looks like beneath the surface. You'll notice the inner parts of you that have been working overtime to keep you safe. You'll see how grief, shame, and unprocessed emotions live in the body. And most importantly, you'll learn to soften judgment; to look at the armor you've worn with compassion, and to honor the part of you that carried you here.

As we move through the process of going *Beyond Numbing,* we are becoming our true selves—the beautiful butterfly who was always waiting inside. This is the first part of that transformation. Think of it as the first wing forming. You'll notice the inner parts of you that have been working overtime to keep you safe, see how grief and shame live in the body, and—most importantly—shift from self-blame to self-compassion.

This quarter of the butterfly reminds us: even in the chrysalis stage, you are already becoming.

CHAPTER ONE

The Many Faces of Numbing

Not all numbing looks the same. For some, it's obvious. For others, it blends in so well that it's praised. Mine learned how to look like responsibility, like over-functioning, achievement, and being the "good girl" who always had it together. These patterns are often celebrated because they look productive, but underneath, they're protective. And deeply exhausting.

As a child, I created an entire world inside my imagination. I would play "house" alone for hours, slipping into stories where I could be anyone, go anywhere, and feel completely safe. I had imaginary friends, Miss Lizzie and Miss Shirley, who went everywhere with me. My mom even held the car door open so they could climb in. They were consistent, kind, and loving. They didn't yell or disappear. They accepted me exactly as I was. My imagination wasn't just a playground. It was a survival mechanism. A sacred place where my nervous system could settle long before I had the words to understand what regulation was.

I grew up learning how to be responsible early. We were latchkey kids, and I took my role seriously. I came home from school, looked after my little brother, folded laundry, and had my homework finished before my dad got home. Not because anyone demanded it, but because I instinctively knew what was needed. I learned how to anticipate, how to manage, how to hold things together. My dad worked hard and did the best he could, but he also leaned on me more than he probably realized. I became the responsible one, the reliable one, the good girl.

My mom coached my teams and showed up in the ways she knew how. Later in life, she came out, a truth that reframed much of my childhood in hindsight. Both of my parents were doing the best they could with what they had, and I learned early how to adapt to the emotional currents around me.

Somewhere between childhood and adolescence, the good girl in me started to unravel. In high school, I dated someone my dad didn't approve of, and his disapproval only made me dig in deeper. It wasn't love, not really. It was control, wrapped in attention. And as someone starved for affection and approval, I mistook that control for connection. My dad and I clashed often during those years. He numbed with alcohol. I numbed with caretaking, performance, and silence.

That's the thing about growing up in a household where numbing is normal. It teaches you how to walk on eggshells. It teaches you who you need to become to stay safe. Sometimes that's the good girl. Other times, it's the rebel. Both versions of me were just trying to survive, be seen and loved.

But numbing wears many masks. It can look like scrolling late at night while your thoughts spiral. Emotional eating—or not eating at all. Cleaning the house obsessively. Sarcasm or giggles as a shield. Control as a comfort. Busyness as a buffer. Smiling when you're breaking inside. It can even look like spiritual bypassing— "good vibes only" when your soul is silently screaming.

Here's the hardest truth. Sadly, numbing works.
It soothes.

It protects.

It gives us space when the world feels too loud.

But it also disconnects us, from our bodies, from our truth, from the very parts of us that need love the most.

For me, it showed up in something as simple as grocery shopping. There were times I'd stock the fridge like we were preparing for an apocalypse. Looking back, I realize I wasn't feeding a family. I was trying to feed a void. That full fridge made me feel full inside. Like I was in control. Like no one would go without. Not on my watch. But the truth was, I was the one running on empty.

That's the thing about numbing. It doesn't always look like shutting down. Sometimes, it looks like overdoing. Over-preparing. Over-giving. Over-functioning. It hides in rituals we call "responsible," while underneath, we're quietly soothing something unspoken.

It took me years to understand that I wasn't trying to be excessive; I was trying to feel safe. And that safety? It was never in the pantry. It was never in perfection. It was in me, waiting to be remembered.

The behaviors you've used to cope weren't the problem. They were the pause button you didn't know you were pressing. But now? You get to choose. You get to stay. You get to meet yourself in the moment—not to fix or perform—but to remember.

You were never too much.

You were never not enough.

You were just protecting the parts of you still waiting to be loved.

And this... is where the healing begins.

Chapter Two

Chaos in Disguise, The Roles We Play

Even when everything looked calm on the outside, my nervous system knew better.

That's the thing about growing up around dysfunction, it doesn't always scream. Sometimes it simmers quietly beneath the surface, shaping how you walk through the world without ever making a sound.

Our home looked "normal" to anyone peeking in. We weren't neglected. There were home-cooked meals, clean clothes, and good grades. But emotional safety? That was harder to come by. And when you grow up in chaos that's hidden or unspoken, it teaches you not to trust your own inner compass. Because nothing around you ever looked like it was broken, you start to believe you're the one who's too sensitive, too dramatic, or too needy. You learn to downplay. To normalize. To absorb discomfort as if it's just the way life is.

Trauma has a funny way of erasing certain memories while locking others in a vault. There are entire stretches of my childhood that feel like static, blurry, or are just... gone. I used to think something was wrong with me for not remembering, but now I understand. When you're not fully in your life, you can't fully record it. Survival mode isn't designed for memory-making.

A dear childhood friend once reminded me that I passed out in the high school hallway. She recalled students circling around me, concerned. I have no recollection of it because my body archived the entire experience. I don't know why I fainted, but I believe it was my body's way of screaming what I couldn't say out loud: *she's not okay.* When you've been living in a heightened state of survival without rest, the body finds its own ways to tell the truth.

And this is where the roles come in. When you're living in quiet chaos, you adapt. You play parts that make life feel a little safer.

I didn't know I was becoming "the responsible one." I didn't wake up one day and decide to be the caretaker, the achiever, or the peacekeeper. It just happened. Someone had to fill in the gaps, and I was already good at sensing what others needed before they said a word.

So, I stepped in. Again, and again. Until that became who I was.

Looking back now, I can name them:

- **The Parentified Child,** managing more than any kid should have to.
- **The Fixer,** trying to make things better for everyone else.
- **The Chameleon,** shifting who I was, depending on the room I walked into.
- **The Peacekeeper,** anticipating needs, avoiding conflict, staying small.
- **The Perfectionist,** tying my worth to my performance, terrified of mistakes.

You may also see yourself in these roles. Do you claim one, or two, of these roles? Perhaps you can see yourself in all of them.

These roles didn't stay in childhood. They followed me into adulthood—into my career, my relationships, and my motherhood. I climbed the corporate ladder carrying a backpack full of unhealed trauma. I wore my responsibility like a badge of honor, never realizing it was also a heavy shield.

In the corporate world, being a high achiever was rewarded. I got the promotions, the recognition, the responsibility, but it came at the cost of my nervous system. I was still that same little girl trying to prove she was enough by doing everything right, by fixing everyone's problems, by performing without ever showing the cracks underneath.

And when I became a mother, the pressure only intensified. The capable one became the *must-be-perfect mother.* When my son was diagnosed with ADHD, I went into overdrive. I became his advocate, his fixer, his shield—because that's who I knew how to be. But no one tells you how lonely it is to be the strong one. The one who always has the snacks packed, the appointments managed, the meltdowns averted. There's no applause for silent suffering. No guidebook for what to do when the role you've played so well starts to feel like a cage.

For most of my life, I didn't know who I was without a role to perform. But roles aren't identities—they're armor. And healing, for me, has meant peeling them off, one by one, until what's left is not a performance, but a person. A mother who can hold space without over-controlling. A woman who no longer must prove her worth by holding up everyone else.

And I'm still on the journey. We all are. Healing doesn't mean the roles disappear. It means we start to recognize them before they take the lead. It means we pause. We get curious. We ask, *"Who's showing up right now—my True Self, or a part of me that learned to perform?"*

Because those roles may have kept us safe...

But they were never meant to be our story's ending.

And the moment we begin to question the performance?

That's the moment we begin to write a new one.

"

NAMING THE
WEIGHT OF
SURVIVAL
IS THE FIRST
STEP TO
SETTING IT
DOWN.

Part Two – Owning the Cost

Every survival strategy has a price. Owning the cost isn't shaming yourself for what's happened, it's finally telling the truth of what it has taken from you.

This is where we turn inward with even more honesty. Once we begin to see the patterns and meet the parts, we can begin to understand where they came from. Not from judgment, but with compassion.

In this section, we'll explore the impact of childhood dynamics, nervous system responses, internalized shame, and the unspoken rules that shaped your self-worth. We'll talk about grief, abandonment wounds, and what it means to unlearn the belief that you were ever broken. You'll begin to see how silence, over-functioning, and self-abandonment may have kept you afloat, but they also left you disconnected from who you really are.

Owning the cost isn't about regret, it's about clarity. And clarity creates space for new choices, new narratives, and a new relationship with yourself.

You're not starting from scratch.

You're returning to your center.

Let's go there together.

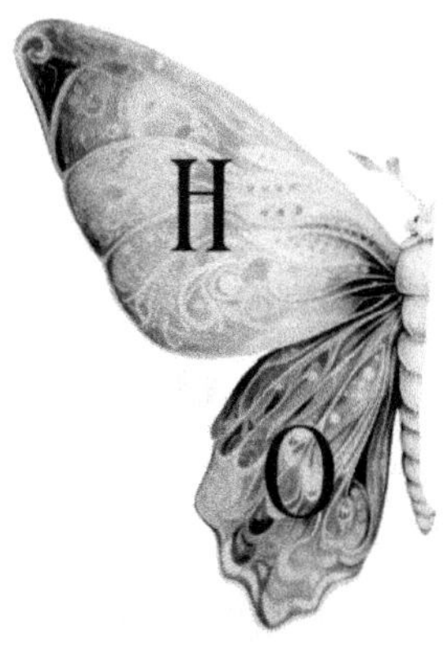

And with that, the second portion of the butterfly begins to take form. The first wing—awareness—has opened, and now the second emerges as we name what survival has cost us. This is the stage where we start to shed the old shell, gently loosening the grip of patterns that no longer serve. Piece by piece, the butterfly takes shape, reminding us that clarity is not the end of the journey, but the unfolding of who we were always meant to be.

CHAPTER THREE

When Trauma Lives in the Body

For years, I thought I was just "high-strung." I believed I had anxiety, maybe some stress, but nothing I couldn't push through. After all, I was functioning. I was achieving. I was doing all the things.

But what I didn't know was that I wasn't just stressed, I was dysregulated. My nervous system had been on high alert for so long that I didn't even recognize what calm felt like, and I wasn't alone. So many of us—especially those who carry childhood trauma—walk around in survival mode and call it our personality.

I thought being "always on," constantly anticipating, and needing to be in control were just parts of who I was. But really, they were symptoms. They were signals from my body, waving red flags and whispering, *"You're not safe. You've never felt safe. You're bracing for what might come next."*

Trauma doesn't just live in our memories. It lives in our bodies. It imprints itself on our nervous system. And when chaos becomes familiar, our baseline shifts. We mistake tension for readiness. We call shutdown "calm." We confuse hyper-independence with strength. And here's what's even more incredible: some of what we carry didn't even start with us.

In a now well-known study, scientists exposed mice to the scent of cherry blossoms while delivering mild electric shocks. The mice developed a fear response to the smell. But what stunned researchers was that their children and grandchildren—who had never been exposed to the shocks—still reacted with fear to that same cherry blossom scent (Dias & Ressler, 2014).

Trauma, it turns out, can be passed down through generations. Through blood. Through biology. Through the invisible wiring of the nervous system. We are not just reacting to our own life experiences. We are often carrying the echoes of what our parents, grandparents, and great-grandparents endured. Their pain, their fear, their coping strategies, they shaped the blueprint we were born into.

Science calls one part of this *epigenetics*, the way trauma and stress can literally change how our genes are expressed. These changes don't alter our DNA itself, but they influence how it's "read" by the body. Children and grandchildren of those who lived through war, famine, or oppression may carry biological markers of that stress. It's not only in the family stories passed down, but also in the body itself.

And then there's the lived reality of generational trauma, which is what we inherit through behavior, beliefs, and nervous system conditioning. A parent who never felt safe may pass down hypervigilance. A family that survived through silence may teach children to swallow their emotions. We inherit not only the biology but also the coping patterns, and survival strategies wrapped in love and pain.

And yet, this isn't about blame. It's about awareness. We are all conditioned by what those before us were taught, and what they were taught was often rooted in survival, not sovereignty. But it can stop with us. We have the power to rewrite the pattern. To regulate what was once dysregulated. To create a different emotional legacy, for ourselves and for the generations yet to come.

Looking back, I can see how many of my behaviors were nervous system responses. You may see yourself in these responses too.

Fawning to avoid conflict.

I apologized even when I hadn't done anything wrong. I laughed off hurtful comments to keep the peace or over-explained myself just to make sure no one was upset. It was all in service of smoothing things over, doing whatever I could to make the discomfort disappear.

Freezing in moments of confrontation.

Hard conversations felt impossible. I'd go completely blank, like I left my body the moment I needed to advocate for myself. The words wouldn't come. I'd either stumble through the moment or go completely silent, retreating into myself.

Overworking to override exhaustion.

My busyness became a coping strategy. I checked emails late into the night because I was convinced I had to stay ahead. Even in moments of rest, I felt uneasy, like productivity was the only way to feel safe.

People-pleasing to secure belonging.

I learned to dim my opinions to fit in. I became whoever I thought others needed me to be, shapeshifting in rooms just to feel accepted. Belonging came at the cost of authenticity.

Even as I climbed the corporate ladder and looked put-together on the outside, inside, I was stuck in a loop of fight, flight, or freeze. No amount of logic or mindset work could help, because my body didn't feel safe enough to let go.

And it wasn't just in the big, dramatic moments. It showed up in everyday situations too, feeling awkward at gatherings, staying quiet; not because I had nothing to say, but because I was afraid of saying the wrong thing. Of being judged. Of being misunderstood.

The quiet ones aren't always shy. Some of us are quiet because we're scanning the room. Reading the energy. Deciding who's safe. Deciding whether it's safe to speak. Silence was my way of self-protection. Of keeping the peace in environments that often felt unpredictable.

Regulation didn't begin for me with breathwork or meditation, though I rely on both. It began with awareness. With understanding that my body wasn't broken, it was brilliant. It had been protecting me all along.

And slowly, gently, I started to build a new relationship with it. One breath at a time, I stopped fighting the fear and started listening to the wisdom underneath it. I started choosing rest before burnout, compassion before perfection, presence before performance.

This chapter of healing doesn't require you to fix everything right now. It only asks that you notice. Because when you notice, you can begin again.

And this time, you get to do it from a place of safety.

From a place of sovereignty.

From your true Self.

CHAPTER FOUR

Unleashing the Lie That You Are Broken

For most of my life, I carried a question like a shadow: "What's wrong with me?"

I couldn't name it, but I felt it everywhere. It was a quiet ache beneath every achievement, every smile, every attempt to prove I was enough. It was as if no matter what I did, something inside me still whispered that I was fundamentally flawed.

That belief didn't come from nowhere. It was learned. Absorbed through years of being told, in subtle and not-so-subtle ways, that I was too much, too loud, not enough, or somehow responsible for the emotions of the adults around me.

And I know I'm not alone in that. So many of us carry invisible scripts that say: *"If someone is upset, it must be my fault."*

We take on the energy of the room. We anticipate moods before they're spoken. We soften our voices, dim our light, or overextend just to keep the peace. And we call it intuition, when really, it's hypervigilance.

That's not sensitivity.
That's survival.
That's trauma conditioning.

When you've been raised to read the room before you speak, you become fluent in emotional safety, but often at the cost of your own truth. You lose your voice. You disconnect from your inner knowing. You start believing that other people's emotions are yours to manage.

Here's what healing has taught me: **That's their energy, not mine.** You can be empathetic without being responsible. Someone else's storm doesn't mean you caused the rain.

It's okay if someone else is in a bad mood. It doesn't mean you need to fix it. You can honor their space without abandoning your own.

Now, when I feel that old pull to absorb what isn't mine, I visualize an energetic shield — not a wall, but a boundary. Like a soft beam of light around me, it lets compassion flow out while keeping other people's projections from seeping in.

That's what boundaries really are. They aren't barriers, but light beams or invisible fences. And as you learn to hold them, you begin to shine steadier. You stop dimming to make others comfortable. You become the lighthouse instead of the sponge.

Because you are allowed to feel peace, even when others do not.
You are allowed to stay grounded, even when others are swirling.

One of the deepest patterns I had to unlearn was hyper-independence. For years, I carried it without even realizing it. I didn't just learn to do things on my own. I needed to. It felt safer that way. I believed doing everything alone was strength. But it wasn't. It was armor. It was the nervous system saying, *"We've got this,"* while quietly bracing for impact. When trust has been broken too many times, self-reliance becomes a safety mechanism.

Even in moments that should have felt relaxing, like watching a movie, I found myself restless. There was always something to do. A task to finish. A mess to clean. A to-do list waiting. Rest didn't feel productive, and it definitely didn't feel safe. Because in a dysregulated nervous system, stillness can feel like a threat. It invites emotion. It invites truth. And for a long time, I wasn't ready to sit with either emotion or truth.

Learning to rest, to soften, to receive, those became radical acts of rebellion and healing. Learning to receive became an act of courage.

I still remind myself daily:
You don't have to earn rest.
You don't have to prove your worth through exhaustion.
You are allowed to exhale.

And then there's this subtle one, accepting compliments. For those of us who've lived with trauma, even kindness can feel suspicious. A compliment can feel like a spotlight, and when you've spent years hiding your worth, being seen can feel unsafe.

So, we deflect, and our responses look like:
"Oh, it was nothing."
"This old thing?"
"I got lucky."

A simple 'thank you' feels oddly vulnerable, like we've let someone see too much. But healing invites us to receive without shrinking. To say *thank you* without the disclaimer. To let love land. A gentle reminder that we can accept kindness without needing to prove, earn, or explain it away.

Every time we allow a kind word in, we remind that younger version of ourselves:
You're allowed to be seen.
You're allowed to be celebrated.
You don't have to disappear to be safe.

I've come to understand that I was never broken. None of us are. We were adapting. Surviving. Doing our best with the tools we had.

Because underneath all the coping, beneath the layers of shame and survival, there has always been a radiant core of wholeness — the light that never went out, even when you forgot it was there.

And that's the invitation now, to stand tall in that light.

To become the lighthouse for yourself, and for others still searching through the fog.

To remember: You were never broken. You were becoming.

Chapter Five

The Parts Within Us

Please note: This chapter is not intended as a clinical guide to IFS or a substitute for therapy. If you're interested in doing parts work or exploring this model in depth, I highly recommend working with a qualified therapist trained in Internal Family Systems.

I used to think there was just one voice in my head, and she was mean.

She told me I wasn't good enough. That I was too emotional, too needy, too loud, too quiet, too much.

She was the one who kept me up at night replaying conversations. The one who cringed at every mistake. The one who pushed me to be perfect and then scolded me when I wasn't.

But when I discovered Internal Family Systems (IFS), everything shifted.

I first learned about IFS through Gabby Bernstein's book *Self-Help*, and something in me finally exhaled. You know those people who don't even realize they've changed your life? Gabby was one of those people for me. Her words introduced me to a model that gave language to what I'd always felt—that I wasn't broken, just layered.

That inner critic I'd fought for years? She wasn't trying to hurt me. She was trying to protect me.

She believed that if I could just be perfect, I'd finally be safe. Loved. Accepted.

IFS revealed to me that we all carry different parts within us, each with a role, a history, and a voice.

These parts are not flaws. They're adaptive. They've helped us survive.

- **Managers** are the ones who keep us in control. The perfectionist, the people-pleaser, the overachiever. They work tirelessly to prevent pain before it happens. They're the part that makes you triple-check the email before you hit send, smile when you want to speak up, or volunteer for one more project just so no one can say you've fallen short. Managers whisper, *"If you stay perfect, they can't reject you."*
- **Firefighters** act fast when pain does arise. They distract us (through scrolling, drinking, shopping, numbing) anything to avoid feeling what hurts. And sometimes, they come out swinging. They're the ones who make us lash out when a lover triggers our deepest fear of abandonment, or when a comment about our children sets off every alarm in our nervous system. In those moments, the anger or sharpness isn't cruelty, it's protection.
- **Exiles** are the younger parts we locked away. The ones still carrying the shame, the grief, the loneliness. The memories we couldn't face. They show up in the tears that spill out of nowhere, in the ache you feel when someone leaves without saying goodbye, in the pit in your stomach when you sense you're being left out. These are the tender parts of us that still believe we are unworthy, unlovable, or unsafe.

Once I saw myself through this lens, everything softened. I could look at the parts I used to hate—the overthinker, the avoider, the one who spiraled in fear—and say, *"Thank you. Thank you for trying to protect me."*

And I began to see them in my own life: the Manager who kept me pushing in my corporate career, afraid to ever fall short; the Firefighter who numbed with busyness and late-night scrolling when emotions felt too heavy; the Exile who held the grief of my childhood, quietly reminding me why trust felt dangerous.

IFS taught me that healing isn't about silencing the noise. It's about listening with compassion. It's about building trust with every part of you. And most of all, it's about letting your calm, curious, confident Self take the lead. And here's the beautiful thing: when that Self leads, the protectors can finally rest. But before they rest, some of them burn things down.

Firefighters act quickly. If they sense you're about to be hurt—or rejected, abandoned, or exposed—they will light the match and walk away. I've felt it in relationships where I said something sharp to create distance. I've shut down emotionally just to feel like I was in control. Because sometimes it feels safer to sabotage something than to risk being hurt by it.

These parts aren't reckless. They're desperate. They've been doing their best to protect us from reliving the pain of the past. But left unchecked, they can scorch the very connection we crave.

That's why learning to respond instead of reacting changes everything. When we pause, notice a part is activated, and say, *"I see you,"* we give ourselves space. We interrupt the autopilot. And we give our Self a chance to lead with love, instead of fear.

Because healing doesn't happen in perfection. It happens in presence.

It's not about fixing every part but about remembering. Remembering that beneath all the roles, all the reactions, all the noise, there is a Self that is calm, capable, connected, and deeply wise.

That part of you?
She never left.
She's just been waiting for you to come home.

Reflection Practice: Meeting Your Inner Parts

I invite you to find a quiet place where you can sit comfortably for a few minutes. Close your eyes, place one hand on your belly and the other hand on your heart. Take a few steady breaths.

Imagine a soft light glowing within you. Imagine it starts in your heart center, radiating out to your entire body. This is a light of curiosity and compassion. It represents your Self, the calm center of who you are.

Now, invite any part of you that wants to be seen to step forward.

There is no need to force or search, simply notice what arises.

You might sense an image, a feeling, a body sensation or a thought.

Ask inwardly:

- *Who's here with me right now?*
- *What do you want me to know?*
- *What are you protecting me from?*

Listen without judgment.
You may meet the part that always tries to fix things, the one that keeps you busy, the one who fears being wrong, or the little one who just wants to be loved. Whatever appears, simply acknowledge it.

Then, place your hand gently over your heart again and whisper:

"Thank you for showing up. I see you. You've always protected me and have helped me more than you know."

Let that part know it doesn't have to carry everything alone anymore — your compassionate Self is here now. Give that part a warm hug of love and envelop them in the healing light radiating from your heart.

Let the other parts come to the stage too. Love them. Thank them. Let them all know they no longer need to protect you.

Take one more deep breath and picture all your parts resting in the warmth of that inner light, connected and calm.

When you're ready, open your eyes.

Maybe jot down a few notes. What did you notice? What surprised you? What did you feel?

Chapter Six

The Weight of Grief and Shame

For a long time, I thought healing meant being happy all the time.

I thought if I could just do enough work—clear enough energy, say enough affirmations, fix all the broken pieces—I'd finally feel peace. But I didn't need to learn how to feel good all the time. I needed to learn how to feel safe. Because after years of numbing, bypassing, performing, and protecting, the idea of feeling my feelings was terrifying.

Grief was one of the hardest emotions to let in.

During the pandemic, my dad was sick. Though I was working from home, leaving California and traveling to Missouri wasn't an option. I did what I could from 2,000 miles away. I talked with him, checked in with doctors and surgeons, helped my brother advocate for his care. I showed up the best I could. But I never felt like it was enough.

When he passed, my protectors kicked into overdrive. My "managers" kept me organized, my "firefighters" numbed me out and my "exiles" stayed buried. I became the strong one. The one pulling it all together. The dynamic with his longtime girlfriend's family was tense, and we were heading into a legal battle over probate that would stretch on for years.

While I was in Missouri for the funeral, I couldn't shed a tear. I was deeply sad, but I couldn't cry. People told me how strong I was.

"Your dad would be proud," they said.

I nodded. I smiled. I thanked them. But inside? I couldn't feel anything. I wasn't just sad, I was numb. Hollow. And underneath the numbness, a quiet shame: *"Why can't I feel the way I'm supposed to?"*

That's what trauma does. It doesn't just shut down pain, it shuts down feeling, period. It's like the emotional circuit breaker trips, and suddenly everything goes dark. It took a long time before I could grieve his passing in a way that felt real.

For months, I gaslit myself: *"What is wrong with you?" "Why didn't you fall apart?"* That is what daughters do when they lose their dad. I sobbed uncontrollably when my Frenchie, Stitch, passed away from cancer, yet I couldn't cry for my father?

That thought haunted me. It became a cruel inner narrative, one that only deepened the spiral.

But what I see now is that my body wasn't broken. It was protecting me. Because sometimes, numbness is what allows us to survive what would otherwise shatter us. Now, from a more grounded place, I can say we have a beautiful relationship. I feel his presence all the time—especially when that deep, full-body feeling of love washes over me. That's how I know it's him. That's how I know love transcends.

Feeling again didn't come through force. It came through safety. Through learning that emotions don't have to overwhelm. That I could stay present without being consumed.

Another layer of healing came in learning to feel safe being alone. Not just physically alone, but alone with my thoughts. For a long time, I equated solitude with abandonment. Silence felt dangerous. Stillness felt like being left behind. Separation anxiety haunted me long into adulthood—and it still creeps in sometimes.

But being alone doesn't mean I've been abandoned. That's a belief I've had to unlearn, again and again. Especially as a mom learning to let go. To give my adult kids space to live their lives without hovering, fixing, or micromanaging. Not being needed in the same way doesn't mean I've lost them. It means they're growing—and so am I.

I'm learning that I don't have to chase connections to feel connected. I don't have to be everything to everyone to be loved. And I don't have to fear quiet moments.

The feelings still come—waves of sadness, fear, uncertainty—but I've learned I don't have to let them take me under. I can feel without drowning. I can witness without collapsing. I can let the emotions move through me without making them mean something about me.

And that, to me, is what healing is. It's the slow, sacred return to everything I once had to turn off and learning, moment by moment, that it is safe to feel it all.

I've walked through the numbness.

Now, I'm learning to stay with myself, no matter what rises.

Grief taught me what it means to survive loss. But shame? Shame was the shadow I didn't even know I was carrying. If grief was the emotion I was afraid to feel, shame was the force quietly shaping how I lived.

Shame doesn't always announce itself loudly.

Sometimes it hides in our politeness, in the way we apologize before speaking. In the way that we overexplain, overperform, or disappear. Shame is sneaky like that. It convinces us we're too much and not enough in the same breath. It tells us to hide the truth of who we are, because if we're fully seen, we might be rejected.

I didn't walk around thinking I felt ashamed. But it was there, in the things I didn't say, in the parts of myself I edited out of conversations. In the way I betrayed my own needs just to be accepted. That's what self-abandonment really is. It's the slow, quiet decision to value someone else's comfort over your own truth. Ugh, how does that statement feel?

I kept secrets, not the kind that get headlines, but the kind that weigh heavy in the body. The kind that sounds like:

"I'm fine."
"It's not a big deal."
"I can handle it."

These were the shields I carried for decades.

Shame in the Corporate World

In corporate life, shame wore the mask of professionalism. I couldn't ask for help—it might make me look unqualified. I couldn't push back—it might make me seem difficult. I was constantly managing how I was perceived, walking that invisible tightrope of being capable but not intimidating, confident but not too much.

I remember once presenting creative layouts to an executive. They weren't what they had envisioned, and instead of offering feedback, they said, "If you can't get the layouts the way I want them, I'll find someone who can." Yikes.

That moment stung—hard. It made me want to turtle in and hide. And for a while, I did. But something else happened too. It lit a fire in me. A quiet determination that said: try again, rise anyway, and never, ever talk to anyone like that. Ever!

That moment taught me a lot about shame, but it also taught me about integrity. I didn't want to lead through fear. I wanted to lead through respect. And just like grief, shame doesn't always break us open with intensity—it seeps in quietly, shaping the stories we tell about who we are and what we deserve.

Shame in Dating and Marriage

In dating, shame whispered that I had to be agreeable to be lovable. That I shouldn't take up too much space or be too opinionated. Or that my boundaries might scare someone away.

And dating after marriage was a whole different story. I carried baggage I didn't even realize was there—stories from my past, fears of repeating old patterns, the quiet question of whether I was still lovable after being broken. Shame told me to hide the parts of me that felt heavy, to tuck away the truth of what I'd been through, as if my past made me less worthy of love in the present.

In my first marriage, shame carried its own conditioning. We bring into our marriages the patterns we inherited from our parents—the roles we watched them play, the dynamics we absorbed without realizing. And when those old dynamics show up in our own relationships, shame convinces us to stay silent.

I used to pride myself on the fact that my ex-husband and I never argued. People would comment on how peaceful we seemed. But the truth was, silence isn't the same as peace. My first husband and I never argued, but we also never opened up honestly. We stayed quiet, not out of harmony, but out of fear that honesty would lead to disconnection.

And when you're raised without boundaries, you bring that baggage straight into matrimony. Without boundaries, love becomes sacrifice. You bend, you shrink, you absorb, until there's very little of *you* left. I thought keeping the peace made me a good partner, when really it was shame keeping me small.

When Shame Creeps In – Even in Love

For a long time, I thought shame only lived in the darker corners of my past — the childhood memories, the people-pleasing, the times I abandoned myself to keep the peace. But what I've learned is that shame doesn't just vanish when you've "done the work." It evolves. It gets subtle. It hides in new layers of your life, even in love.

I'm married to my twin flame — my person. The one who sees me on a soul level. And yet, there are still moments when shame shows up between us, quietly, unexpectedly.

It's the moment I snap, then immediately feel guilty for not being the "healed" version of myself.

It's the discomfort that rises when he offers help and I feel undeserving of being cared for. It's the tension in my chest when I fear I've disappointed him, even when he hasn't said a word.

That's the tricky thing about shame: it doesn't always announce itself. It whispers through body language, tone, and silence. It tells us stories like, *"You should've known better,"* or *"You're too much,"* or *"You don't deserve this kind of love."*

But I've come to understand that being in a conscious, spiritual partnership doesn't mean you never trigger each other. It means you learn to recognize when shame is in the room, take a breath, and name it before it takes over.

Sometimes I'll literally say to myself, "That's my shame talking." It's a simple phrase, but it brings me back to truth. Because when shame is named, it loses its power. It transforms from a hidden wound into an invitation for connection.

My marriage has become a mirror. Not to reflect my flaws, but to show me where I still get to soften, where I still get to receive, and where I still get to practice being loved without earning it.

Healing doesn't mean you stop meeting your shadows. It means you meet them with open eyes and a softer heart. Even when they show up beside the person who loves you most.

Shame in Parenting

As a mom, shame crept in constantly. When I lost my temper. When I forgot something. When I compared myself to other moms who looked like they had it all together. Shame told me that one wrong move would ruin my kids forever.

I believed good moms didn't yell. Good moms didn't struggle. Good moms never needed help.

But we don't parent in a vacuum. We parent from our conditioning. And when you grow up as a parentified child—the strong one, the perfect one, the one who never caused waves—you carry that into motherhood. You enable so your kids don't fail. You make sure they never go without. You over-function, because that's what once kept you safe. But in trying to protect them from every stumble, you deny them the chance to grow.

What I've come to realize is that perfection isn't what our kids need. They need presence. They need honesty. They need to see that it's okay to repair and return. They need to be heard, to be seen, and yes, even to fail sometimes.

I'm reminded of my own wisdom in the *ABCs of Self-Love: A Journey to Rediscovering Yourself,* it's not about quantity, it's about quality. Our children don't need us to do everything. They need us to be someone they can trust to show up as real, not perfect. Modeling grace with myself teaches them more than always getting it "right."

Shame in Comparison

And then there's the kind of shame that thrives in silence: comparison shame. The kind that bubbles up when we scroll through someone else's highlight reel. When their family looks happier. Their home looks cleaner. Their marriage looks stronger. We wonder, *"What's wrong with me? Why can't I be more like that?"*

That's the thing about shame; it doesn't just silence us. It isolates us. It makes us believe we're the only ones struggling while everyone else is thriving.

When we live in shame, we also live in lies. We lie to ourselves. We lie to our families. We lie to our friends. Not because we're dishonest, but because maintaining the illusion feels safer than confronting the truth. We hide behind smiling photos and polished stories while quietly falling apart. And over time, those lies become a lifestyle.

But isn't that the cruelest cycle of all? A cycle that feeds itself, one that never ends until we consciously choose to stop it? Until we decide to tell the truth, even when it's uncomfortable—especially when it's uncomfortable?

It's easier to wear a mask than to face the shame within. Easier to become someone we think others will approve of than to reveal the parts of ourselves that still feel unworthy.

But healing asks us to take off the mask.

And when we begin to do that—when we start telling the truth to ourselves first—we begin to build something new: self-trust.

Self-trust doesn't arrive all at once. It builds slowly, through small acts of self-honoring. For me, it started with a self-care routine. Not the Pinterest-perfect kind, but the kind that whispered, *you matter*. The kind that reminded me I was worthy of care, even when no one else was watching.

When you start to consistently show up for yourself, something powerful happens—you begin to believe your own presence. You realize that if you can't trust yourself to meet your own needs, it becomes nearly impossible to trust others to do it either.

And here's the truth that took me years to learn. Self-trust is the foundation of every other kind of trust. And when self-trust begins to rise, so does your voice.

Not the performative one, but the true one—the voice buried beneath the roles, the rules, and the silence you were taught to keep.

That voice?

She's coming home.

"

HEALING ISN'T PERFECTION,
IT'S A PROCESS.

ONE THAT ASKS YOU TO PAUSE,
BREATH AND BE PRESENT WITH
THE WHOLENESS ALREADY
INSIDE YOU.

MOMENT BY MOMENT.

BREATH BY BREATH.

Part Three – Pause in the Healing

There were so many P's that I couldn't decide on just one. Process, Pause, Presence—they all belong here. Each one offers something vital for this stage of transformation.

Process reminds us that healing is not a one-and-done moment. It's a slow unfolding, a step-by-step return to ourselves. Every time you recognize a pattern and choose differently, you're in the process of becoming.

Pause invites us to stop rushing past our own needs. To give the nervous system space to exhale. It asks us to rest before burnout, to soften before we collapse, to notice instead of numb.

Presence is the grounding that makes it all possible. It's the practice of being here, now—not stuck in the regrets of the past or the fears of the future. Presence is what allows joy, freedom, and color to return, even in the midst of imperfection.

Together, these P's carry us deeper into integration. They teach us to stop abandoning ourselves and start creating a life that feels safe for us. They remind us that wholeness doesn't come from performance—it comes from peace.

Reclaiming the Self doesn't mean you never fall back into old patterns. It is about recognizing them sooner. You extend grace to yourself. You choose differently. You stop abandoning yourself to keep others comfortable, and you start creating a life that feels safe for you.

This is the remembering. This is the rising. Let's keep going.

At this stage, you are three-quarters of the way through your transformational butterfly. You've crawled as the caterpillar, surrendered in the cocoon, and now you're beginning to sense your wings forming. You're not quite ready to fly, but you're no longer crawling either. This is the in-between, the process of strengthening, of pausing, of practicing presence. And it's here that you gather what you need to step fully into embodiment in the final stage.

CHAPTER SEVEN

The Tug-of-War Within

There comes a point on the healing path where you stop asking, *"What's wrong with me?"* and start asking, *"Who was I before the world told me I had to be someone else?"* That's the moment you begin to reclaim your True Self.

It doesn't always arrive with fireworks. Sometimes, it's quiet. Sometimes it's as subtle as hearing your own voice in a still room and realizing, *"I've missed her."*

You begin to notice that the version of you who held everything together wasn't you. She was the protector. The performer. The perfectionist. The peacekeeper. She was the one who knew how to keep you safe when the world didn't feel safe. But underneath all of that? There's someone softer. Braver. Freer. Someone who existed before the shame, before the masks, before the world said, *Be less. Be nice. Be quiet.*

For me, disconnection often looked like avoidance. Not that anyone seeks out conflict, but avoiding it altogether is toxic. If I told myself that my dad wasn't an alcoholic, then he wasn't. If I told myself my marriage wasn't falling apart, then it wasn't. I had mastered the art of stuffing down feelings that felt too hard to process. In some ways, it was a gift—one I relied on for survival. But deep down, I knew it was costing me the truth of who I was. The internal struggle was real.

And yet, when I finally honored my voice—when I made the hardest decision of my life and chose to put myself and my kids on a different track—that was when the new path revealed itself. Divorce wasn't easy. It shattered the illusion I had carefully built. But it also opened the door to alignment, to safety, to a life that finally felt honest. I haven't looked back.

That's the paradox of healing. It's the moment we choose truth over avoidance, our protectors panic. My manager parts whispered, *"Don't stir things up. Keep it together."* My firefighters urged me to distract myself, to bury the grief and carry on. My exiled parts trembled with fear of abandonment. But beneath all those voices, the True Self was whispering, *"Trust me."* And when I listened, even in the smallest ways, I realized she had been there all along.

Reclaiming the True Self isn't about becoming someone new. It's about remembering who you were all along. Sometimes that remembering begins in stillness—therapy sessions, journaling, long drives without music, quiet mornings when the noise falls away. Sometimes it comes in moments of courage, when you speak the truth that you've been silencing for years.

The more I leaned into authenticity, the louder the old voices became. *"You're fine. Don't open that door. Don't be dramatic. Who do you think you are?"* Those weren't the voices of truth. They were the echoes of fear. The healing came when I began to ask myself, *"Which voice is rooted in fear, and which is rooted in love?"* Because the True Self doesn't shout, panic, or shame. She whispers through alignment. She reminds you of your worth without requiring a performance.

A Practice: Heart-Based Decisions

When you notice conflicting voices inside—fear on one side, longing on the other—place your hand on your heart and ask:

If I choose from fear, what does it feel like in my body?
If I choose from love, what does it feel like in my body?

Your ego will argue. Your parts will strategize. But your heart never lies. It speaks with simplicity, with calm, with clarity. And the more you practice listening, the more you'll recognize the voice of your True Self.

Reclaiming your voice is only the beginning. The next step is learning how to use it (in the presence of others) without shrinking, people-pleasing, or performing. That's where trust begins. Not just in yourself, but in the world, you're creating by finally showing up as who you truly are.

This is the stage of the butterfly where you're emerging from the cocoon. The wings are fragile, the body unsteady, and flight is still ahead. But you are no longer hidden. The True Self is rising, and with every small act of trust, you strengthen the wings that will soon carry you into freedom.

CHAPTER EIGHT

Living in Alignment

Once I started to trust myself, I realized how hard it still was to trust other people. There are times I still struggle with this now. Not because everyone was untrustworthy, but because I had spent so many years keeping myself safe from disappointment, abandonment, and betrayal. Trust had become a risk I wasn't sure I could afford.

When you've been hurt by the people who were supposed to love you, when your childhood teaches you that love is conditional, inconsistent, or absent altogether, you don't just stop trusting them. You stop trusting yourself. So even when someone safe comes along, you question it. You brace yourself. You wait for the letdown. That's what trauma does. It stores the past in your body and keeps you bracing for something you can't name.

For me, the "strong, independent woman" who never asked for help was also the little girl who had learned not to expect it. Vulnerability felt dangerous. Asking for support felt like being a burden. It was safer to do it all alone than to risk needing someone who might let me fall. But here's the truth I had to learn is that people can't love the version of you that you keep hidden.

Trust is a bridge, rebuilt slowly—plank by plank—with communication, consistency, and courage. I remember early in my relationship with my husband, we took our first trip away together. We were still getting to know each other, still learning how to feel safe in real time. At one point, he stepped out to grab something from the car, and without thinking, I blurted out—half joking, half not— "Don't leave me here." He turned, confused. "Why would I leave you here?" I laughed it off, but inside, the moment stayed with me. Because even when everything felt okay, some part of me was still holding my breath.

That's the thing about trauma—it lingers in your nervous system. You don't have to feel unsafe to still be bracing. Healing meant learning that trusting others isn't about ensuring no one will ever hurt me again. It's about knowing that if they do, I'll handle it. I'll grieve. I'll grow. I'll move forward. Because I am solid in myself. That's what gives me the strength to open my heart again, not naively, but wisely. Not everyone gets access. Not everyone deserves it. But the ones who show me, through actions and not just words, that they are safe, consistent, and respectful. That's where trust can finally bloom.

And this is where alignment begins. Because living in alignment isn't just about trusting others, it's also trusting yourself enough to honor your boundaries, your energy, and your truth.

For so long, I didn't know the difference between survival and alignment. I thought I was thriving because I was busy, because I was needed, because I was achieving. But I wasn't living on purpose. I was living for approval.

Boundaries became the first bridge. Learning to say no without apology. To stop overexplaining myself. To honor my time, my energy, my capacity. Boundaries aren't walls; they're invitations to connection with clarity. They protect what matters most: our peace, our purpose, our self-worth.

But setting them wasn't easy. Not when my identity was tangled up in being the dependable one, the liked one, the one who could do it all without breaking. And yet, each time I said yes to myself—especially in small, almost unnoticeable ways—I laid a stronger foundation beneath me.

Then came the spiritual connection. That quiet remembering that I am not doing this alone. That I am supported, guided, and deeply loved by something greater. Some call it Source, God, the Universe, the Higher Self. I personally call on God Himself. And when I began to tune in, I started seeing signs. Feeling nudges. Experiencing moments of divine timing that reminded me: I am not lost. I am led.

This connection didn't make me feel smaller, it made me feel safer. It helped me trust myself more deeply. I stopped outsourcing my worth to how others responded. I started listening inward instead of constantly reaching outward. I began asking not just *"What do I want to do?"* but *"What am I being called to do?"*

Looking back, I realize how early I was taught to disconnect from my intuition. As a child, I had moments of spiritual awareness that were quickly dismissed. When I saw things others couldn't explain, I learned to doubt myself. When I felt things deeply, I was told to move on. Slowly, I stopped trusting the voice within.

Healing invited me back. Back to the knowing. Back to the unseen. Back to the girl who always felt things deeply, even when others didn't understand. Now, as an adult, I honor what was once dismissed. I embrace what was once called strange or scary. I call on my divine counsel every day. I know, without a doubt, I am being guided.

Spirituality became the ground beneath me. It steadies me on the hardest days. It lifts me when I feel lost. It reminds me that I am never doing this alone. Purpose didn't come like a lightning bolt. It arrived in layers. In whispers in every sacred "yes" to what lights me up, and every brave "no" to what drains my soul. It revealed itself in the ordinary. In the way I held space for clients, in the chapters I dared to write, in the truths I finally spoke aloud after years of silence.

Living with purpose doesn't mean having it all figured out. At its core, it's being rooted in who you are, guided by something higher, and fiercely protective of what matters most. It still requires boundaries. It still requires faith. It still requires course correction. But it feels different. It feels like coming home.

To your voice.
To your power.
To your path.

This is the life I was always meant to live. Not from fear. Not from proving. But from truth. From soul. From alignment. And that changes everything. We weren't born to live numb. We were born to live aligned.

And that's the invitation I want to leave you with. Because healing isn't just about fixing yourself—it's about becoming the lighthouse you were always meant to be. A steady presence. A grounded light. A quiet beam that doesn't chase the ships but guides them home by standing tall in its own place.

When you live aligned, you don't just find safety for yourself. You become safety for others. You show them that it's possible. That it's safe to shine. And that there is always a way through the dark.

CHAPTER NINE

When Loving Yourself Changes Everything

The most life-altering moment of my healing journey wasn't a sudden breakthrough or a spiritual awakening under the moonlight. It was quieter than that. It was the slow, deliberate decision to love myself—fully, unapologetically, and without waiting for someone else to show me how. And perhaps the bravest act of that self-love was choosing divorce.

Letting go of the relationship I had once believed would be forever wasn't just about leaving a marriage. It was about coming home to myself. It was about recognizing that staying small, unseen, and unfulfilled for the sake of comfort or appearances wasn't love. It was survival.

It was also about showing my kids that choosing yourself isn't selfish. It's sacred. I wanted them to see what it looked like to honor your truth, even when it came with sacrifice. Divorce didn't just mean two households—it meant co-parenting through seasons of uncertainty, stretching every dollar, and sometimes saying no to things that other families took for granted. We didn't have a TV for a while, but instead of that being a loss, it became a gift. We filled our time with "real talk," with board games, long drives, laughter in the kitchen, and simply being present together. Those moments taught us quality over quantity, connection over consumption.

Now, as adults, they see it. They understand the freedom that came with my choice. They recognize the strength it took to leave a life that looked fine on the outside but felt hollow on the inside. And they see the difference in me. The mama who raised them was loving, yes, but also surviving—busy, tired, keeping it all together because that's what she thought she had to do. The mama they know today lives differently. I'm still the same woman physically, but I no longer parent from exhaustion or fear. I lead by example, choosing alignment and truth over performance and perfection. The woman who sacrificed her own needs to keep the peace is gone. In her place is a mother who shows them, through her own life, that strength and vulnerability can exist side by side.

But the lesson of self-love didn't stop with them. Showing my kids a new way forward also meant learning to walk that path myself. Because loving yourself isn't just about what you give to others, it's more about what you're willing to let yourself receive. And for me, that was the hardest part.

At first, I didn't trust it. I questioned it. I rejected compliments. I waved off kind gestures. I scanned even healthy relationships for the red flags I'd grown so used to. Love felt foreign. Uncomfortable. Even unsafe. Because when you've spent years building walls to protect your heart, it's disorienting to let someone in and realize they're not trying to hurt you.

Letting love in takes practice. It takes discernment. It takes learning to trust your body when it says this is safe and having the courage to believe it. And it's not just romantic love. It's allowing friends to show up for you. It's receiving support without guilt. It's believing that your voice belongs in the room. It's letting the divine love of God's grace flow through you, not just around you, so you can be YOU.

I used to think self-love was bubble baths and boundaries. And yes, sometimes it is. But more often, it's standing in the mirror with grace instead of criticism. Because the truth is, we are often our own worst critics. We zero in on the muffin top over our jeans or the lines on our face and say things to ourselves we'd never allow another person to say. We defend against harshness from others, but too often we invite it in from within. And here's the part we forget: our inner child is always listening. Every cruel thought, every whispered insult, every "not enough" burrows into her heart.

Self-love begins when that inner narrative changes. When we speak to ourselves with the same gentleness we longed for as children. When we stop tearing ourselves apart and start practicing the radical act of kindness toward the person in the mirror. That's where the shift truly begins.

Loving yourself changes everything because it resets the standard. You stop chasing crumbs when you realize you deserve the whole table. You stop shrinking to be loved when you realize love expands you. I've learned that trust doesn't mean others will never hurt you. It means you trust yourself to handle it if they do. That's the real safety. That's what allows you to love fully—without losing yourself.

Not everyone earns a place at your table. But when you've healed enough to know your worth, you learn how to choose those who do. Letting love in is no longer something I fear. It's something I cherish. Because every day I choose to love myself a little more, I make more space for love in every form.

That's the gift of healing. Not just surviving. Not just being strong. But being soft enough to receive. And whole enough to know you're worthy of it all. And when you show up as your full self—unmasked, unfiltered, and unafraid—the love that finds you isn't just real. It's aligned.

"

FREEDOM ISN'T
FOUND IN BECOMING
SOMEONE NEW, BUT
IN REMEMBERING
WHO YOU ARE."

Part Four – Embodying Freedom

This final section is about integration—the embodiment, the becoming, and the practice of living whole. Healing isn't a destination where life is suddenly perfect. It's a daily choice, a commitment to yourself, a way of being rooted in alignment, authenticity, and truth.

This is the moment the butterfly takes flight—not because you transformed into someone unrecognizable, but because you finally trust the wings you've carried all along. Living beyond numbing means honoring your energy, even when it's low. It means noticing when you want to disconnect and gently calling yourself back. It means setting boundaries without guilt, resting without shame, and loving without fear of being too much.

The world will still test you. There will be days when your nervous system whispers fear, when self-doubt creeps in, and when the outside noise feels louder than your own voice. But now you have tools. You have awareness. You have a relationship with yourself that's rooted in truth. You know how to come home to yourself, to choose presence over performance, peace over perfection, alignment over approval.

And as you do, you're not only living differently, you're leading differently. You're breaking cycles with your presence. You're showing your children, and your children's children, that it's okay to be seen, to be messy, to be real. You're living proof that wholeness makes room for it all—your softness and your strength, your humanity and your divinity.

You've come so far. And the path ahead is yours to walk with grace, with courage, and with love. This isn't the end. It's the unfolding of everything you were always meant to be.

The butterfly in her fullness isn't fragile anymore. She's radiant, wings spread wide, showing colors and patterns that were hidden all along. She doesn't look back at the cocoon in regret. She honors it as part of her becoming. What once felt constraining has now given her the strength to fly. And flight isn't about escape, it's about presence, about moving through the world with beauty, with grace, and with purpose.

That's the invitation of this final section. To not only know you're healing, but to embody it so deeply that others can feel it. To live as the butterfly does—in the freedom of who you truly are, unafraid to take up space, unafraid to be seen, and unafraid to fly.

CHAPTER TEN

Real Connection Requires the Real You

Healing changes your relationships, not always because people leave, but because you change.

When I began walking a more spiritual path, something unexpected happened. I didn't go around cutting people out, but some quietly stepped back. My healing made others uncomfortable. My connection to the divine, to energy, to intuition? Some labeled it "woo-woo" and didn't understand it. Some still don't.

I've learned that you don't need everyone to understand your path for it to be valid. Your spiritual journey is yours. Sacred. Deeply personal. And it doesn't require anyone else's stamp of approval.

There comes a moment in your healing when you realize:

- If you have to shrink to be loved, it's not love.
- If you have to perform to be accepted, it's not connection.
- And if you have to wear a mask to belong, you'll never feel truly seen.

Real connection doesn't come through perfection, it comes through presence and presence requires truth. There's a loneliness that hits differently when you're surrounded by people but still hiding. The size of the circle no longer matters, it's whether you feel safe being your full self inside it.

I remember being at dinner parties, laughing at jokes I didn't find funny, nodding through conversations that honestly drained me. I'd come home and collapse on the couch, wondering why I felt so lonely when I was constantly surrounded by people. The truth was, I wasn't lonely for others, I was lonely for myself.

Even in my marriage, there were seasons where I confused surface harmony for true intimacy. I'd check the boxes—date nights, daily texts—but still feel a quiet ache beneath it all. Because real connection isn't about consistency; it's about honesty. And for years, I was afraid to be fully honest about what I needed, what I felt, or who I was becoming.

I had to unlearn the habit of self-editing—of laughing when I wasn't okay, of avoiding topics that made others uncomfortable, of morphing into who I thought someone needed me to be just to avoid judgment or rejection. Because when you live like that long enough, you forget who you are underneath it all.

Healing stripped away the superficial. I stopped chasing people who invited me to parties and started noticing the people who made me feel safe in silence. I began valuing eye contact over small talk, presence over performance. It's funny how so many of the things I once thought mattered no longer do. The right outfit, the perfect reply, the unspoken competition of who has it more together? It all feels hollow now.

The older I get, the more I crave simplicity. Depth. People who ask how your heart is, not what you're working on. People who make you laugh until you forget your phone exists. That's the currency of connection I value now.

The turning point for me was realizing I couldn't keep calling in aligned friendships, relationships, and opportunities while showing up as a filtered version of myself. Real connection requires the real you. And yes, that comes with risk. Not everyone will understand. Some will leave. Some will say you've changed.

But others? They'll exhale. They'll lean in. They'll whisper, *"Thank you for saying what I didn't know how to put into words."*

That's when I learned the powerful truth that your full, unpolished, unapologetic self isn't too much. It's medicine for someone else's silence.

Not everyone has earned access to your vulnerability. Discernment isn't about being guarded, it's about being wise. You don't owe your full story to everyone. But you do owe your truth to yourself. And when you start showing up in your life as the real you—not the version people prefer, but the version that's been rising all along—the connections that remain are the ones worth keeping.

Your presence is your power. Your truth is your compass. And the moment you stop filtering yourself to be palatable is the moment you become magnetic.

And maybe that's what spiritual growth really does—it pulls you out of the noise and into the sacred. It makes you notice the sound of your own laughter, the warmth of your own presence, the quiet peace of being exactly who you are. Connection stops being about who stays or leaves and becomes about how deeply you're willing to stay with yourself.

CHAPTER ELEVEN

The Power of Your Voice

I wasn't silent because I was shy. I was silent because I was scared.

For so many years, I read the room before I spoke. I weighed my words carefully, filtered my thoughts, and prioritized everyone else's comfort over my own truth. And even now—with all the work I've done—I still notice that little girl inside me. The one who scans the room for safety. The one who wants to make sure it's okay to speak.

She's still here. But she doesn't lead anymore.

Because my voice matters. And so does yours.

The power of your voice isn't about volume, it's about truth. It's about using your story not as justification or apology, but as a beacon. A reminder to others that they're not alone. A hand extended in the dark.

That's what I've come to understand. I didn't go through all this just to survive it. I went through it so I could speak to it. So, I could stand up and say, *"There's another way."*

There's also a moment on the healing journey when you realize your pain had a purpose. That all the inner work—the unraveling, the reparenting, the releasing—wasn't just for you. It was also preparing you to be a safe space for someone else.

At first, I thought my role was to fix. To offer answers. To be the solution. But what I've come to understand is real healing doesn't come from being rescued, it comes from being witnessed.

When I first began coaching one-on-one, my fixer parts were still running the show. They meant well, but what they were really avoiding was the discomfort of sitting with someone in their pain. It took time—and my own continued healing—to see the truth: transformation isn't tidy. People don't need you to clean up their pain. They need you to honor it.

Now, I don't see myself as a healer. I see myself as a facilitator. A guide. A mirror. Someone who walks beside you as you return to yourself. The more I trusted that role, the more powerful the work became. My story—the chaos, the conditioning, the climb—has become my offering. I share it so others know they're not alone.

And that's where the real power of voice comes in.

Sharing my truth through my writing, coaching, and speaking isn't about spotlight. It's about service. My mission now is to help others recognize their own patterns of numbing, disconnection, and self-abandonment, and to create a safe space for their healing to begin.

Yes, I'm still a work in progress. I still catch myself shrinking sometimes, second-guessing, reverting to old conditioning. But now I *see* it. I catch it sooner. I gently remind myself that it's safe to speak. It's safe to be seen. It's safe to take up space. And every time I share my voice with courage, even when it trembles, I show that little girl inside me just how powerful she's always been.

Perhaps the most powerful part of reclaiming your voice is realizing that you're not just healing for yourself. You're healing for the generations that came before you and the ones that will come after. When I speak my truth, when I show up authentically—even when it's messy—I'm showing my children and my children's children that it's okay to be human. That it's okay to feel. That it's okay to ask for what you need and to take up space in this world.

We break generational trauma not by being perfect, but by being real. By saying, *"This ends with me."* By being the first to speak when silence was once the rule. By creating a new pattern that gives the next generation permission to live unfiltered, unmasked, and fully expressed.

This is how we become cycle breakers—not through control or performance, but through presence, voice, and truth.

And this voice?

It was never lost.

It was simply waiting for me to remember it was mine.

Yours is in there too. And when you're ready to use it, it will rise.

CHAPTER TWELVE

We Break the Cycle Here

Every family carries stories, some spoken, some silent. And for many of us, it's the silence that speaks the loudest - the unhealed grief, the shame that was swallowed, and the coping that turned into patterns.

I grew up carrying the weight of cycles I didn't create. Addiction. Codependency. Silence that kept the truth tucked away in the shadows. And like so many daughters, I inherited not just my parents' love, but also their pain.

There were years I thought that's just how it had to be, that I couldn't escape what ran in my blood. But what I know now is this: trauma may be handed down but so can healing. Cycles don't just continue. They also break.

And they break here. With *me*. With *you*. With anyone brave enough to say, *"It ends now."*

Breaking cycles doesn't mean you never stumble. It doesn't mean you suddenly parent perfectly or never repeat an old pattern. What it means is that you live with awareness. That you choose to pause where others reacted. That you repair where others avoided. That you tell the truth where silence once reigned.

For me, that looked like shifting how I parent. I didn't, and don't, always get it right. I remember the first time I caught myself repeating my father's tone; sharp, clipped, and laced with frustration. The words left my mouth before I could stop them, and my daughter's eyes filled with tears. The shame hit me hard, but instead of shutting down, I took a breath and did something different. I apologized. Not as the all-knowing parent, but as a woman learning.

That was the moment I realized breaking cycles doesn't happen in grand gestures. It happens in those small, humbling moments when you choose connection over control.

As a parentified child, I grew up believing my worth was tied to being perfect, to never causing waves. I carried that into motherhood by hovering, fixing, and ensuring that my kids never failed. But healing showed me that what they needed wasn't my performance of perfection. They needed my presence. They needed to see me repair, to see me be human, to see me love myself enough to stop abandoning my truth.

And it hasn't only been about my children. Breaking cycles has also meant turning toward my own inner child. The little girl who thought she had to hold everything together. I've learned to listen to her, nurture her, to remind her that she is safe now. There are days I still feel her tug. The part of me that wants to keep the peace, fix the problem, or hold it all in. When she shows up, I pause. I place a hand on my heart, and I whisper, *"You don't have to be the hero anymore"*. That is what reparenting really is. Learning to give yourself what you've always given everyone else: grace, patience, tenderness and truth.

Generational healing doesn't happen in grand ceremonies; it happens in the quiet, daily choices that look ordinary but are anything but. It happens in choosing to rest instead of overperforming. In telling your story instead of keeping it buried. In saying *no* when silence would've been easier.

When you choose to heal, you're not just changing your life, you're rewriting the story for those who came before you and those who will come after. You're showing your children, your grandchildren, your community that it's safe to be real. That it's safe to feel. That it's safe to love without losing yourself.

We don't break cycles by being perfect. We break them by being present.

By staying when the instinct is to run.
By softening when we want to armor up.
By telling the truth, even when our voices tremble.

That presence—that courage—that willingness to live differently?
That's the legacy worth leaving.

Because when we heal, the butterfly doesn't just take flight for us. She carries every generation touched by our wings. And maybe that's what true freedom really is—learning to love so fully, so honestly, that the next generation doesn't have to heal from our silence.

CHAPTER THIRTEEN

Becoming Her: Living Unapologetically

Integration isn't the end of the journey. It was the doorway into something deeper. Becoming her means living the truth you spent years uncovering.

But who is *she?*

She's not a new version of you. She's the *YOU* that's always been there beneath the fear, the roles, and the conditioning. She's the woman you've been remembering—your authentic, grounded, fully expressed self. The one who trusts her own voice, who honors her energy, who no longer performs for approval.

Becoming her isn't about striving to become someone else. It's about peeling back everything you were never meant to carry so the real you can finally breathe. It's the moment your healed-self and your higher-self become one.

This is no longer just *talking* about boundaries, it's about *holding* them. It's not just reading the books and doing the meditations; it's embodying the lessons when life throws you curveballs. It's trusting your worth even when no one else claps for you.

Becoming her means honoring your energy unapologetically. These days, my team knows I go to bed early. There are nights I just want to crawl under the covers, and because I can't stay in bed long without falling asleep, I'm out by 9. I value my sleep, and that may mean emails don't get answered.

"Amie is already out," they tease.

And you know what? I love that for me. Because that's what self-honoring looks like now. It's reclaiming what I need and not apologizing for it.

But becoming her also means embracing the messy middle. Healing doesn't always look radiant. It's learning to feel your emotions without letting them drown you. It looks like giving yourself grace when you're a hot mess. It looks like catching yourself when old patterns creep back in and lovingly choosing to return home to yourself.

Let's be honest, this part seems easy from the outside. All those memes about "protecting your peace" and "releasing what no longer serves you" make it sound effortless. But it's not. Not when you've spent a lifetime people-pleasing and prioritizing everyone else's needs over your own. Not when your nervous system has been wired to avoid conflict at all costs.

Living unapologetically isn't about being loud or brash but being rooted. It's walking through the world anchored in who you are, even when others don't understand it. There will be people who get upset when you set boundaries because they were the ones who benefited from you not having any. There will be people who try to manipulate you, twist your words, or gaslight your truth. That's their coping mechanism. That's their unhealed stuff. And while they might try to blame you for their behavior, that doesn't mean you have to put up with it.

You'll encounter moments that make you question yourself. *"Am I being too soft?" "Am I letting this person get away with something?" "Am I being too harsh?"*

It can feel like an internal tug-of-war. But living unapologetically is trusting your own internal compass. It's remembering that kindness is not the same as being a doormat. It means learning that your softness is strength and so is your voice.

And there's another layer; the spiritual one. Living unapologetically also means living in spiritual alignment with your soul, your higher self, and your divine mission. Healing may have led you here, but it's spiritual surrender that allows you to stay.

It's trusting divine timing, even when life tests your patience. It's letting your intuition speak louder than your fear. It's calling on your divine counsel and remembering you're not doing this alone. You're co-creating with something greater. That means honoring the whispers of your soul even when they don't make sense to the world around you.

When I look back, I can see how my imagination was my first teacher in co-creation. As a child, it gave me a place to go when the world felt unsafe. A space where I could dream myself into safety, softness, and freedom. That wasn't weakness; it was wisdom. My mind was already learning how to create safety from within.

What I once used to survive, I now use to expand. The imagination that built protective worlds back then is the same one that now builds possibility. Healing has taught me that daydreaming is sacred, that it's simply visualization wrapped in innocence. The visions we once used to escape become the ones that help us embody the life we're meant to live.

Manifestation is such a buzz word now and it's important to know that it isn't about forcing outcomes. Manifestation is about aligning your energy with what your soul already knows is possible. When we imagine our future selves and feel her joy, peace, and confidence in our body now, we begin to live from that frequency. That's when reality starts to shift.

The little girl who once imagined safety was practicing embodiment before she even knew the word. And today, she still whispers reminders: *You already know how to do this. You've always been the dreamer. You've always been the creator.*

This version of you? She honors her needs. She protects her energy. She no longer over-explains or justifies her boundaries. She doesn't twist herself to be palatable. She lives with intention. With trust. With spiritual alignment.

Becoming her isn't about a perfect version of you but becoming more *you* than you've ever been. Soft and strong. Boundaried and loving. Rested and radiant. A woman who listens to her own voice first. Who trusts her timing. Who knows she's allowed to take up space, to rest, to laugh loudly, to say no, and to change her mind.

This version of you? She was always there. You're just finally allowing her to lead.

And that's what it means to live unapologetically. Not perfectly, but intentionally. With grace. With self-respect. With the sacred knowing that you were never too much, you were simply too much for the spaces that asked you to be less.

Chapter Fourteen

Beyond Numbing: A New Way Forward

Living in alignment with your divine self doesn't mean floating through life in a permanent state of zen. It means remembering, repeatedly, who you are beneath the fear, the conditioning, and the noise. It means returning to that sacred place within you where truth lives. Where your soul speaks. Where you know you are guided.

And let's be real, some days that's easier said than done.

There are moments when my phone goes on *Do Not Disturb*, not because I'm avoiding people, but because I need to protect the pocket of time that I've carved out to journal or meditate. There are nights when I crave stillness and quiet, when Amie is simply "out" for the evening. Not because I'm shutting people out, but because I'm finally honoring my own rhythms.

This is what living beyond numbing looks like in practice. It isn't always rituals or crystals or sage. It's the daily choices that bring you back to truth. It's listening for the whisper of your Higher Self over the noise of doubt. It's trusting the nudge, following the guidance, and co-creating with the Universe—even when it feels scary.

Alignment also means recognizing what no longer belongs. It's remembering that the people who bristle at your boundaries are the very ones who benefited most from you not having any. It's standing tall when someone tries to twist your truth or manipulate you into believing their toxic behavior is your fault.

Living in alignment is a daily practice. Even after all the work, you'll still encounter judgment, resistance, and triggers. You'll still hear the old whispers: *Maybe you're too much. Who do you think you are?* But now, you know how to come home to yourself. You know how to answer.

Your divine self doesn't demand perfection, she invites presence. She reminds you that your softness is not a flaw, but a gift.

That your intuition is not silly, but sacred.
That your rest is not lazy, but necessary.

This version of you walks with faith, not because she is fearless, but because she is finally listening to the voice within.

Integration is where the nervous system softens, the inner child feels safe, and the Higher Self begins to lead. It's the quiet strength that says: *I will continue to show up for myself, not because I am broken, but because I am worthy.*

Healing often arrives in subtle ways, showing up as the pause before reacting, the breath before speaking, or the quiet moment when you notice the old story rising and choose not to follow it.

Spiritual surrender has been one of my greatest teachers. When I stopped gripping so tightly—trying to control, predict, and prove—I discovered that I wasn't meant to carry it all alone. I began to trust that I was guided. That love, not fear, was at the center of who I am.

And yet, life is still life. Distractions, comparisons, and old narratives still show up. Some days I fall into them, but integration means noticing sooner. Returning with kindness. Offering myself grace instead of judgment.

This journey has never been about perfection—it's about presence. About staying with yourself when things feel messy. About knowing that your softness is strength, your rest is sacred, your joy is your birthright.

This book was never just a book. It was a remembering. A reclaiming. A return.

Numbing was never the destination—it was a survival strategy. The armor you wore until you had the tools to feel. And now, you do.

Beyond numbing is where life begins again. It's where you meet your emotions without fear of drowning in them. Where you speak your truth without apology. Where you rest without guilt. Where you let yourself be seen, unmasked, unfiltered, and whole.

As a child who grew up in a home touched by addiction, I've come to understand something deeply: the behaviors we judge—alcoholism, eating disorders, overworking, people-pleasing—are not the root wounds. They are coping strategies. Signals of pain we were not ready to face. When we meet them with compassion instead of shame, the true work of healing begins.

Living beyond numbing means coming home to yourself again and again.
Through the breath that steadies you.
Through the boundaries that protect your peace.
Through the rituals that keep you grounded in truth.
Through the courage to let yourself be loved.

You are not broken. You are not behind. You are a cycle breaker, a truth-teller, a soul who remembers.

So, live it. Call on your divine counsel. Trust the wisdom of your soul. Let your Higher-Self lead.

Not perfection, but devotion.
Not arriving, but allowing.
Not performing, but being.

This is the way forward—beyond numbing.

The Empowered Self

You made it. And for me, this was never just words on a page. It was a remembering of everything I had to forget to survive, and everything I've since reclaimed to live fully. It was a return to myself. To love. To wholeness.

If you've made it this far, it means you were willing to walk with me. To sit in the discomfort, to face what's been buried, and to let the light in anyway. That takes courage. Healing is not a straight line; it's a spiral of returning to yourself, again and again. And every time you do, you rise a little higher, grounded in a deeper truth.

You've walked through the numbness and faced the ache. You've met the parts of yourself you once hid, and you've come to realize that healing was never about fixing what was broken. It's always been about remembering what was whole.

Through this journey, you've peeled back layers of protection that once kept you safe and begun to see the patterns that kept you small. You've learned to pause before reacting, to speak your truth without apology, and to hold yourself with the compassion you once reserved only for others. You've recognized that the stories you inherited are not the ones you have to keep living, and that awareness alone changes everything.

Empowerment doesn't arrive in a single defining moment; it builds slowly, through presence and practice. It's not loud or perfect—it's quiet and steady. It's the inner knowing that you no longer need permission to take up space in your own life.

The Empowered Self isn't someone you become one day: she's the version of you who's been patiently waiting underneath the noise. She's the voice that whispers, *you already know.* She's the calm that finds you when you stop running, and the strength that rises when you finally allow yourself to rest.

The Empowered Self is my everything. It's the message woven through every word of this book, the heartbeat of my newsletter of the same name, and the purpose behind every meditation, course, and conversation I share. It's not just a concept; it's a way of living—a daily return to truth.

It's the reminder that empowerment isn't about striving to be more; it's more about remembering who you already are. It's about coming home to yourself, again, until it feels natural to live from that place.

Your healing doesn't end here—it evolves. It expands every time you choose peace over performance, truth over pleasing, and softness over self-protection. You're no longer surviving; you're creating. You're leading. You're becoming the lighthouse—shining your truth not to save others, but to remind them they can find their own way home. The world needs your light, your softness, your boundaries, and your voice.

As you move forward from here, may you remember that you are not behind—you are becoming.

You are not broken—you are blooming. And you were never meant to play small.

You are *The Empowered Self,* the embodiment of everything you once thought you had to chase.

Keep choosing you. Keep coming home. Because this journey doesn't end—it deepens.

With so much love,

Amie

Sources & Further Reading

The concepts, stories, and teachings in this book are rooted in personal experience, lived healing, and years of both formal and informal study in trauma, generational patterns, emotional wellness, and nervous system regulation.

The following works, studies, and frameworks helped inform and support the ideas presented throughout these pages.

Scientific Research & Articles

Cherry Blossom Trauma Study

Dias, B.G., & Ressler, K.J. (2014). *Parental olfactory experience influences behavior and neural structure in subsequent generations. Nature Neuroscience, 17*(1), 89–96. https://doi.org/10.1038/nn.3594 (Referenced in chapters discussing generational trauma and epigenetic imprinting.)

The Body Keeps the Score

van der Kolk, B. (2014). *The Body Keeps the Score: Brain, Mind, and Body in the Healing of Trauma.* Penguin Books. (Referenced for understanding how trauma affects the body and nervous system.)

Nervous System & Somatic Healing

The Polyvagal Theory

Porges, S.W. (2011). *The Polyvagal Theory: Neurophysiological Foundations of Emotions, Attachment, Communication, and Self-Regulation.* W.W. Norton & Company. (Referenced in discussions of safety, regulation, and connection.)

Accessing the Healing Power of the Vagus Nerve

Rosenberg, S. (2017). *Accessing the Healing Power of the Vagus Nerve: Self-Help Exercises for Anxiety, Depression, Trauma, and Autism.* North Atlantic Books. (Referenced for practical somatic and vagus nerve–based tools.)

Inner Work, Parts Work & Self-Compassion

Internal Family Systems (IFS)

Schwartz, R.C. (2021). *No Bad Parts: Healing Trauma and Restoring Wholeness with the Internal Family Systems Model.* Sounds True. (Referenced for understanding parts work, Self-leadership, and compassionate internal dialogue.)

Self-Compassion

Neff, K. (2011). *Self-Compassion: The Proven Power of Being Kind to Yourself.* William Morrow. (Referenced for foundational work on self-kindness, emotional awareness, and resilience.)

Generational Healing & Emotional Inheritance

It Didn't Start With You

Wolynn, M. (2016). *It Didn't Start with You: How Inherited Family Trauma Shapes Who We Are and How to End the Cycle.* Penguin Life. (Referenced in discussions on generational wounds, patterns, and healing cycles.)

Spiritual Growth & Emotional Resilience

Self Help

Bernstein, G. (2024). *Self Help: This Is Your Chance to Change Your Life.* Hay House.
(Referenced for her grounded, spiritual approach to personal transformation.)

Acknowledgements

There are so many beautiful souls who contributed to bringing this book into being, beginning with my husband, Brian. Your unwavering support has been the steady ground beneath me, the quiet strength that gives me the courage to keep going.

To my children, Heston and McKenna — thank you for allowing your mama to make difficult decisions you didn't always understand, but that were necessary for me to become the woman and mother you deserved.

And to Kaitlin, Brianna, and Jacqueline — thank you for welcoming me into your lives with open hearts. You didn't know me when my healing journey began, yet you embraced my "woo woo" ways, and took me in as your own, and I am forever grateful.

To Hanna Olivas — thank you for being the guiding light who helped me recognize my voice, my truth, and my potential.

To the incredible "Inkubator" sisters — Sylvia Becker-Hill, Sonya McDonald, Erica Elliot, Carmen Maendel, and JoAnn Nider — your love, wisdom, and encouragement carried me long before this book ever began to take shape.

And to every person who has crossed my path throughout this journey — whether for a season or a lifetime — you played a role in my growth, healing, and expansion. For each moment, lesson, and connection, I am eternally grateful.

About the Author

Amie Rich is an author and speaker devoted to helping others break free from generational patterns and come home to themselves. A certified high-performance coach, spiritual hypnotherapist, and nervous system practitioner, Amie blends science with emotional healing and spiritually grounded practices to guide individuals on their journey from survival to self-love.

After nearly three decades climbing the corporate ladder while quietly battling people-pleasing, burnout, and inherited trauma, Amie stepped into her own deep healing. What began as a personal unraveling became a profound calling: to help others release the patterns that keep them numb, small, and disconnected from who they truly are.

Her work is rooted in compassion, lived experience, and the belief that healing radiates forward — transforming not only ourselves, but the generations that follow. Through her books, courses, meditations, and energy healing sessions, Amie supports others in regulating their nervous system, trusting their intuition, and reclaiming their worth.

She lives in Southern California with her family, where she continues to write, create, and uplift a growing community of individuals ready to choose themselves again.

Disclaimer

This book is not a clinical manual and is not intended to replace professional support. While every effort has been made to offer accurate and thoughtful guidance, the content within these pages is meant to educate and inspire you on your personal journey toward inner peace and emotional well-being.

I am not a psychologist, therapist, or medical doctor. I do not offer psychological, medical, or health advice. If you are experiencing a psychological or medical condition, please seek support from a qualified mental health or medical professional.

Please note that the suggestions, reflections, exercises, and practices in this book are based on general healing principles and may not be suitable for every individual. Use discretion and always honor your own intuition and personal safety.

The author and publisher are not responsible for any actions taken as a result of reading or applying the information provided. The intention of this book is to offer insight, support, and education of a general nature to assist you on your emotional, physical, and spiritual journey. Should you choose to use any of the information for yourself, you do so at your own discretion, and the author and publisher assume no liability for your choices or outcomes.

If this book resonated with you, I want you to know something…

You don't have to figure out the next step on your own.

Healing doesn't happen all at once. It happens in small, supportive moments when you're given space to pause, feel, and reconnect with yourself in a way that feels safe.

I've created additional resources to support you beyond these pages, including:

- The Empowered Meditation Library. A gentle, nervous-system-supportive place with guided meditations, EFT tapping scripts and more to help you find your inner peace.
- **Several self-reflection ebooks and workbooks** to help you integrate what you've uncovered here

If you'd like to explore what's available, you're invited to visit my website **amierich.com.**

You'll find offerings designed to meet you where you are, whether you're just beginning to soften out of survival mode or ready to deepen your self-trust.

There is no rush.
No right timeline.
Just the next honest step.

With care,
Amie